JUST ADD WATER

SCIENCE PROJECTS YOU CAN SINK, SQUIRT, SPLASH, SAIL.

Children's Press®
An Imprint of Scholastic Inc.
New York Toronto London Auckland Sydney
Mexico City New Delhi Hong Kong
Danbury, Connecticut

Book production: Educational Reference Publishing

Book design: Nancy Hamlen D'Ambrosio

Science adviser: Jennifer A. Roth, M.A.

Library of Congress Cataloging-in-Publication Data

Just add water : science experiments you can sink, squirt, splash & sail.
    p. cm. — (Experiment with science)
  Includes bibliographical references and index.
ISBN-13: 978-0-531-18545-2 (lib. bdg.)   978-0-531-18762-3 (pbk.)
ISBN-10: 0-531-18545-1 (lib. bdg.)   0-531-18762-4 (pbk.)
  1. Water—Experiments—Juvenile literature. 2. Water
chemistry—Juvenile literature. I. Children's Press (New York, N.Y.)
II. Title.
GB662.3.J87 2008
546.22 078—dc22
                              2007021682

1 2 3 4 5 6 7 8 9 10   R   17 16 15 14 13 12 11 10 09 08

SOC CONTENTS

Hard or Soft?

How can water be "hard" or "soft"? Let suds show you the answer.

Underwater Volcano

What happens when hot and cold water collide? An underwater volcano will show you.

Meltdown!

Learn how salt and sand stop you from slip sliding away.

Drip, Drip, Drip

Find out all about stalactites and stalagmites and how they form.

Layers of Liquid

Oil and water don't mix. In this experiment, you'll find out why.

Hair Humidity

Make a hair hygrometer, and learn the science behind those bad-hair days.

Float Your Boat

Find out what keeps a big boat afloat!

Rainmaker?

Create a mini-version of Earth's water cycle—and make it "rain" inside.

Why Don't Fish Sink?

Make a scuba diver that sinks and floats before your eyes.

JUST ADD WATER

Water covers most of the planet Earth. In fact, more than 70 percent of Earth's surface is covered by water. Oceans and seas, lakes and ponds, and rivers and streams contain water in its liquid state. But that's not all! Water in its solid state, ice, covers another 10 percent of Earth in the Arctic region and Antarctica. Still, there's more! The clouds overhead contain water, too, in its gas state, called water vapor. Is this making you thirsty? No wonder! Your body is more than two-thirds water!

Each experiment in this book leads you through the steps you must take to reach a successful conclusion based on scientific results. There are also important symbols you should recognize before you begin your experiment. Here's how the experiments are organized:

Name of experiment

Goal, or purpose, of the experiment

A **You Will Need** box provides a list of supplies you'll need to complete the experiment, as well as the approximate amount of time the experiment should take.

Here's What You Will Do gives step-by-step instructions for working through the experiment.

Here's What's Happening explains the science behind the experiment—and what the conclusion should be.

Mess Factor shows you on a scale of 0 to 5 just how messy the experiment might be (a good thing to know before you begin!).

MESS FACTOR: 3

Science Safety: Whenever you see this caution symbol, read the instructions and be extra careful.

What is water? Water is made up of the elements hydrogen (H) and oxygen (O). In a molecule of water, there are two hydrogen atoms (H_2) and one oxygen atom (O). $H_2 + O = H_2O$. What makes water so special? Scientists would say that water is special because of the way its elements are attached, or bonded, to one another. It is this unusual type of bonding that gives water its special properties. Sound complicated? It's not, really—and you can see for yourself. The experiments in this book will help you understand the amazing wonders of water. You'll do experiments that show what dissolves in water and what won't dissolve—no matter what. You'll see what happens when water freezes . . . and you'll be amazed at what happens when hot and cold water meet. To find out more, turn the page and dive in!

This symbol means that you should ask an adult to help you or be nearby as you conduct the experiment. Although all the experiments in this book are appropriate and safe for kids to do, whenever you're handling anything that might be sharp or hot, it's important to have adult supervision.

In the back of the book, **Find Out More** offers suggestions of other books to read on the subject of water, and cool Web sites to check out. The **Glossary** (pages 30-31) provides definitions of the highlighted words appearing throughout this book. Finally, the **Index** is the place to go to find exactly what you're looking for.

Here are some important tips before you begin your experiment:

- Check with an adult.
- Read the experiment all the way through.
- Gather everything you need.
- Choose and prepare your "lab" work area.
- Wash and dry your hands.
- Use only clean containers for your experiments.
- Keep careful notes of everything you do and see.
- Stop and ask an adult if you aren't sure what to do.
- When you're finished, clean up your work area completely, and wash your hands!

HARD OR SOFT?

WHAT MAKES WATER HARD OR SOFT? MINERALS. IN THIS EXPERIMENT, YOU'LL FIND OUT HOW HARDNESS AFFECTS WATER'S SOAPING AND DISSOLVING POWER.

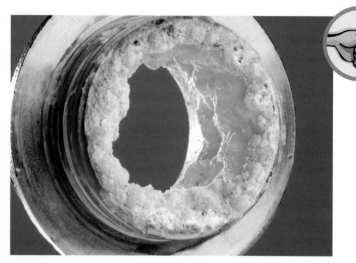

Hard water causes blue minerals to form on the inside of this copper piping.

YOU WILL NEED

- ❑ 3 large bowls
- ❑ distilled water
- ❑ tap water
- ❑ spoon
- ❑ 1 box Epsom salts
- ❑ 1 bar of soap
- ❑ sink
- ❑ towel

TIME:
15 MINUTES

HERE'S WHAT YOU WILL DO

MESS FACTOR: 3

1 Fill one bowl with distilled water that you've warmed in the microwave. Fill two bowls with warm tap water. Add a spoonful of Epsom salts to one of the tap-water bowls.

2 Wet your hands with the plain tap water. Spend five seconds (count slowly!) lathering them up with soap. Notice how much suds you make.

Rinse off your hands at the sink. Note how long it takes to rinse off *all* the soap.

Epsom-salts water   plain tap water

Dry your hands. Repeat the above steps with the distilled water and then the Epsom-salts water. Dry your hands thoroughly in between. How sudsy did your hands get? How long did it take to rinse away the suds?

HERE'S WHAT'S HAPPENING

In nature, water picks up minerals as it moves through the ground. The more minerals it picks up, the "harder" the water becomes. The minerals in hard water combine with soap and prevent the soap from making a lot of lather. As a result, you get fewer soap bubbles and more of a soap scum on your hands. Bathtub rings are examples of hard-water scum. So is the film on your hands after washing with Epsom-salts water. Distilled, or purified, water is "soft," because the minerals have been removed, so your hands get very soapy when you lather up!

distilled water

MELTDOWN!

IN THE WINTER, SALT AND SAND ARE USED TO PREVENT CARS FROM SLIDING ON ICY ROADS. IN THIS EXPERIMENT, YOU'LL SEE THE EFFECTS OF SALT AND SAND ON ICE AND FIND OUT ABOUT THE FREEZING POINT OF WATER.

This truck is throwing a mixture of salt and sand that melts snow and provides traction on icy roads.

 ## YOU WILL NEED

- ❑ 3 large ice cubes
- ❑ 3 saucers
- ❑ teaspoon
- ❑ 1/2 teaspoon salt
- ❑ 1/2 teaspoon sand
- ❑ clock or watch

TIME: 20 MINUTES

Freezing Water

Freshwater freezes when its temperature drops below 32° F (0° C). Ocean water, which is about 3 percent salt, remains liquid until its temperature drops below 28.5° F (-1.9° C). The saltier the water, the lower its freezing point. Salt water consisting of 23 percent salt remains liquid until it reaches -6° F (-21° C). *Brrrr.*

MESS FACTOR: 2

HERE'S WHAT YOU WILL DO

Place a large ice cube (at least an inch square) on each of the three saucers.

Pour half a teaspoon of salt on one ice cube. Pour the same amount of sand on another. Leave your third ice cube as is.

After 10 minutes, observe the cubes. Which has melted the most? Rub your finger across the surface of each cube. Which is the least slippery?

HERE'S WHAT'S HAPPENING

Frozen salt water melts at a colder temperature than does frozen freshwater. So when the salt dissolves on the ice cube, the cube melts faster. Sand doesn't dissolve in water. So it doesn't affect the cube's freezing point. But sand has other advantages on icy surfaces: it can provide more traction—or antislipping power—than salt does. Sand is also less harmful than salt to plants and animals.

LAYERS OF LIQUID

WHY DOES OIL FLOAT ON TOP OF WATER? IN THIS EXPERIMENT, YOU'LL FIND OUT ABOUT THE DENSITY OF LIQUIDS.

Oil and water don't mix. Oil is less dense than water, so it sits on top of the water.

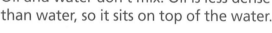 YOU WILL NEED

- ☐ 1/2 cup water
- ☐ food coloring
- ☐ measuring cup
- ☐ clear drinking glass or jar
- ☐ 1/2 cup corn syrup
- ☐ 1/2 cup vegetable oil
- ☐ marble
- ☐ small rubber ball
- ☐ paper clip
- ☐ other small objects (optional)

 TIME: 15 MINUTES

 MESS FACTOR: 2

HERE'S WHAT YOU WILL DO

1 Add a few drops of food coloring to a half cup of water. Pour it into the glass or jar. Next, add a half cup of corn syrup. Does the syrup sink beneath the water?

2 Gently pour a half cup of the oil into the glass. Does it float on top of the water?

3 Drop the small objects into the glass one at a time. In which of the three layers does each object settle?

HERE'S WHAT'S HAPPENING

Have you ever noticed how the oil and vinegar in salad dressing separate into layers inside the bottle? This is because the vinegar has a greater density than the oil. Density is the measure of how much matter is packed into a volume, or space. To measure something's density, scientists compare it to the density of water at room temperature, which has a density of 1.

Oil is less dense than water, so it floats on top of water. Corn syrup is denser than water, so it sinks to the very bottom of your jar—below the water. Solid materials have different densities as well. The density of the objects that you dropped into the jar are different too. The less dense objects rest in the top two layers. The denser objects sink to the bottom.

FLOAT YOUR BOAT

A BALL OF CLAY SINKS IN WATER, BUT A CLAY BOAT—EVEN LOADED WITH "CARGO"—FLOATS! IN THIS EXPERIMENT, YOU'LL SEE HOW AN OBJECT'S SHAPE CHANGES ITS ABILITY TO FLOAT.

This heavy cargo ship floats because its surface is spread out across the water.

YOU WILL NEED

- ☐ 1 strip of modeling clay
- ☐ bowl of water
- ☐ several pennies or marbles

TIME: 20 MINUTES

MESS FACTOR: 1

HERE'S WHAT YOU WILL DO

1 Roll the clay into a ball about an inch wide. Drop it into the water. Drop a few marbles or pennies into the water. They all sink, right?

2 Take the clay out of the water and shape it into a small bowl, or "boat," with a wide bottom and high sides. Place it into the water. It floats!

3 Gently place a few pennies and marbles into the boat, one at a time. Does the boat settle a little lower in the water with each addition of cargo? Does it eventually sink?

EUREKA!

The idea of buoyancy, or the ability to float, is also called the Archimedes Principle. The Greek mathematician and inventor Archimedes (illustration at left) discovered this law of physics some 2,200 years ago when he sat down in his bath and noticed that his body caused the water level to rise. The more water an object displaces, he realized, the more buoyant it is. According to scientific lore, Archimedes was so excited by his discovery that he rushed out into the street, without getting dressed, shouting "Eureka!"—which means "I've got it!"

WHAT'S A PLIMSOLL LINE?

A ship never completely floats on water. A part of it is always beneath the water's surface. How much below the surface of the water depends on the ship's weight. The Plimsoll line is a mark on a ship's side (see the photo at right) that shows the deepest level that a ship can safely sink into water. If the water level goes above the Plimsoll line, the ship is too low in the water. . . and it could sink.

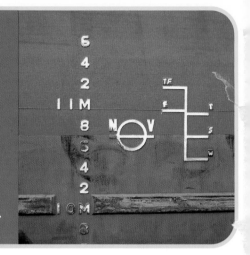

HERE'S WHAT'S HAPPENING

In the previous experiment, you learned that objects and liquids will sink through water if they are denser than water. In this experiment, the clay's weight didn't change when you re-shaped it. But by hollowing out the clay, you created an object that spread out across more water surface. Objects float if they weigh less than the volume of water they push aside. The wider the bottom and sides of your boat, the more water it displaces and the more buoyant, or better able to float, it becomes. Adding cargo increases a boat's weight. When it weighs more than the amount of water it displaces, the boat will sink.

WHY DON'T FISH SINK?

WHAT KEEPS FISH FROM SINKING TO THE BOTTOM OF AN AQUARIUM? HOW DO DIVERS AND SUBMARINES CONTROL THEIR UNDERWATER DEPTH? MAKE A MODEL SCUBA DIVER AND FIND OUT THE ANSWERS!

Controlling buoyancy is one of the most important skills for divers to master.

YOU WILL NEED

- ❑ pen cap with pocket clip
- ❑ 1 strip of modeling clay
- ❑ glass
- ❑ water
- ❑ 2-liter soda bottle with cap
- ❑ heavy aluminum foil (optional)
- ❑ glue (nontoxic; optional)

 TIME: 30 MINUTES

MESS FACTOR: 3

HERE'S WHAT YOU WILL DO

1 If the top of your pen cap has a hole, plug it completely with a bit of modeling clay. Add a larger piece of clay to the tip of the cap's pocket clip.

2 The cap will be your "diver." You can give it a human (or fish!) form by cutting a figure out of heavy-duty aluminum foil and gluing it to your pen cap. Be sure the glue is completely dry before getting it wet.

3 To be sure that your diver floats, lower it into a glass of water with the opening of the pen cap facing down. (A bubble of air will remain inside the cap. This will keep the diver from sinking.) You want the cap to float just high enough so that its tip touches the water surface. Add more clay if it floats too high. Remove some if it sinks too low.

COOL FACT!

Most fish control their buoyancy with a special gas-filled organ called a swim bladder. The swim bladder is located in the upper part of the fish's body, below the kidney and above the intestines. Sharks don't have this organ. This is one reason why sharks have to keep swimming all the time. Otherwise they'd sink!

4. Fill the large plastic bottle full of water, leaving just a tiny amount of air on top. Lower your scuba diver inside before tightly screwing on the lid. Now squeeze the sides of the bottle. Can you control your diver's depth with the strength of your squeeze?

HERE'S WHAT'S HAPPENING

When you squeeze on the sides of the bottle, you increase the pressure inside. The increased pressure reduces the size of the air bubble inside the pen cap, allowing a little more water to enter it. This decreases your diver's buoyancy.

Deep-sea divers wear ballast compensators, inflatable vests that expand with air or let air out. Submarines work in a similar way. To rise in the ocean, air is pumped into their ballast tanks. The tanks are flooded with water to dive back down.

UNDERWATER VOLCANO

BY CREATING AN UNDERWATER VOLCANO, YOU'LL DEMONSTRATE THAT LESS-DENSE LIQUIDS FLOAT ON TOP OF MORE-DENSE LIQUIDS.

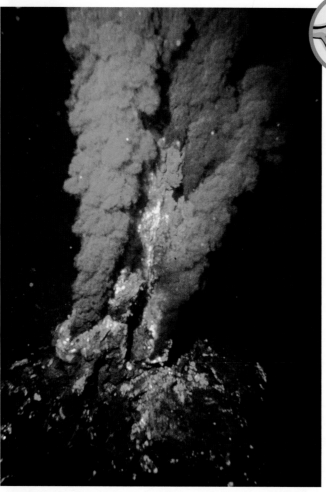

Hot-water volcanoes exist in nature, too. They're called deep-sea vents. They shoot up from the floor of the ocean when heat from the earth and the cold seawater collide.

 YOU WILL NEED

- ❑ scissors
- ❑ 1-2 feet of string
- ❑ small, narrow-necked glass or plastic bottle
- ❑ large, wide-mouth glass or plastic jar
- ❑ water (hot and cold)
- ❑ food coloring

TIME: 30 MINUTES

ADULT

HERE'S WHAT YOU WILL DO

1 Cut a long piece of string. Tie both ends to the neck of the small bottle to form a handle. (Any small, glass container with a wide bottom and a narrow neck would work well.)

2 Fill the large jar three-quarters full with cold water. Make sure its mouth is wide enough to "swallow" your smaller bottle.

3 Ask an adult to fill the small bottle with hot (but not scalding) water. Add several drops of food coloring to get a bold color.

4 Hold the string handle, lower the small bottle into the large jar, and watch!

HERE'S WHAT'S HAPPENING

When water is heated, its molecules start moving apart. So there are fewer of them in a given space. In your volcano, the hot water erupted up and out of the bottle because the hot water was less dense, or lighter, than the cold water around it. The molecules in a cold liquid remain clumped together because they have little energy. When energized by heat, the molecules start moving. If you add enough heat, the molecules will even start flying into the air as water vapor!

DRiP, DRiP, DRiP

STALACTITES AND STALAGMITES ARE MINERAL DEPOSITS THAT FORM IN CAVES AND CAVERNS. IN THIS EXPERIMENT, YOU'LL CREATE SIMILAR UNIQUE FORMATIONS.

The slow dripping of water over thousands of years forms the stalactites and stalagmites in caves.

YOU WILL NEED

- ❏ 2 medium-size jars
- ❏ warm tap water
- ❏ 1 box Epsom salts
- ❏ spoon
- ❏ baking pan or serving tray
- ❏ scissors
- ❏ 1 foot of thick yarn
- ❏ 2 nails
- ❏ ruler

 TIME: 3-4 DAYS

 **MESS FACTOR: 4**

HERE'S WHAT YOU WILL DO

1 Fill both jars about three-quarters full with very warm water (hot, but not scalding). Add **Epsom salts** a spoonful at a time while stirring to dissolve as much as you can in each jar. Depending on the size of your jar, you might need a cup or more. Place the jars about 5 inches (13 centimeters) apart on the baking pan.

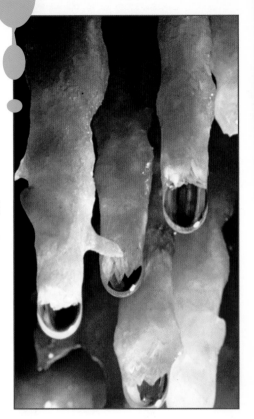

2 Cut a piece of yarn about 1 foot (.3 meter) long. Tie a nail to each end. Place one nail into each jar so that the end of each string reaches the bottom of its jar. Adjust the distance of your jars so that the middle of the string droops between them, but remains at least an inch or two above the pan.

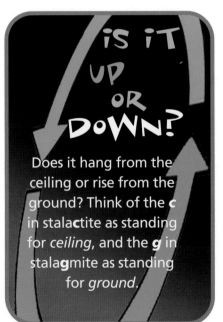

IS IT UP OR DOWN?

Does it hang from the ceiling or rise from the ground? Think of the **c** in stala**c**tite as standing for *ceiling*, and the **g** in stala**g**mite as standing for *ground*.

3 Observe your experiment each day for several days. Is a **stalactite** forming on the string? Is a **stalagmite** growing below it? You might even get more than one of each. Each day, for three days, record their lengths on a table like the one on the next page.

HERE'S WHAT'S HAPPENING

When the water in the jars evaporates into the air, the Epsom salts form crystals around the string. As more water evaporates, more crystals cling to the yarn or drip to form a pile on the pan. This is similar to the process that created the strange mineral deposits called stalactites and stalagmites that occur in a cave or cavern.

These crystal deposits formed over thousands of years as mineral-rich water dripped down into the cave from the ground above. As each water drop clung to the ceiling of the cave, it left a tiny ring of limestone mineral around its entry point and a matching splash of lime below. Over time, the lime formed a little stone "icicle" on the ceiling (stalactite) and a "stubby candle" (stalagmite) on the ground directly below it.

Stalactite

Stalagmite

HAIR HUMIDITY

HUMID AIR CAN GIVE YOUR HAIR THE FRIZZIES. USE YOUR OWN HAIR TO MAKE A HYGROMETER— AND LEARN THE SCIENCE BEHIND SOME OF THOSE BAD-HAIR DAYS!

Humid air contains a lot of moisture, and it can make hair extra curly and frizzy.

YOU WILL NEED

- ruler
- pen
- index card
- 4 pushpins
- corrugated cardboard
- sewing needle
- drinking straw
- 1 strip of modeling clay
- 9" strand of straight hair
- tape

TIME: 1 WEEK

MESS FACTOR: 1

HERE'S WHAT YOU WILL DO

1 Line up your ruler along the edge of an index card. Draw a scale that matches the 1/4-inch marks on the ruler. (See the photo at right.) The scale should be vertical (straight up and down). Attach the index card to the cardboard with your pushpins.

2 Push the needle through the straw 1 inch (2.5 centimeters) from the straw's end. With the straw attached, stick the needle into the cardboard. The opposite end of the straw should cross over the scale as shown in the photo.

3 Balance the straw with a small amount of clay on the end away from the scale. Adjust the amount of clay until the straw balances horizontally (parallel to the ground) when the board is sitting up straight.

4 Pluck one hair (not a bunch!) from your head or, with permission, from the head of someone with long, straight hair. Trim it to around 9 inches (23 centimeters), and tape one end to the straw between the clay and the needle. Tape the bottom of the hair to the bottom of the cardboard. You now have a working hygrometer!

5

Set your hygrometer upright in a humid room such as a bathroom where a hot shower has been running. Wait about 20 minutes. Mark where the straw crosses the scale. Repeat in a cool, dry place. Or gently dry the hair with a blow-dryer on low. Again mark where the straw crosses your scale. Is there a big difference?

6

Leave your hygrometer undisturbed for a week or more. Each day, mark the straw's position on the scale with a small notation of the date. You will likely see a difference in humidity levels from day to day.

HERE'S WHAT'S HAPPENING

So why does some hair get the frizzies in humid weather? Air contains many different gases. One of these gases is water vapor. Humidity is the measure of how much water vapor is in the air. In dry air, human hair loses water and shrinks. In humid air, hair absorbs water and expands. Besides powering your hygrometer, this quality tends to make some hair curly or frizzy on a humid day.

RAINMAKER?

WHERE DOES RAIN COME FROM? IN THIS EXPERIMENT, YOU'LL DEMONSTRATE HOW WATER CYCLES BETWEEN EARTH'S SURFACE AND THE ATMOSPHERE HIGH ABOVE US.

Rain begins as water vapor in a cloud. It is an important part of Earth's water cycle.

YOU WILL NEED

- ❏ measuring cup
- ❏ 3/4 cup dry dirt
- ❏ small plastic cup
- ❏ large, clear glass bowl
- ❏ water
- ❏ plastic cling wrap
- ❏ rubber band (optional)
- ❏ ice cubes
- ❏ sealable sandwich bag
- ❏ strong sunlight or gooseneck lamp

TIME: 1-1/2 HOURS

MESS FACTOR: 3

HERE'S WHAT YOU WILL DO

1 Pour the dirt into the bottom of the cup. (An empty, serving-size yogurt container works well.)

2 Place the cup into the middle of the bowl. Fill the area around it with an inch or two of water. (Avoid getting water inside the cup.)

3 Snugly, but not too tightly, cover the bowl with the plastic wrap. Make sure the entire rim is sealed. You can stretch a rubber band around the rim if you have trouble getting a good seal.

4 Place a large ice cube (or several smaller ones) into the sandwich bag, seal the bag, and fold it around the ice cube. Place it on top of the plastic wrap, directly above the cup. Gently press down on the ice so the plastic wrap above the cup sags a little.

5 Set the bowl in strong, direct sunshine near a window. Or use a gooseneck lamp as your Sun—bending the neck so the bulb shines about 16 inches (41 centimeters) from the side of the bowl.

6 Check back in about an hour. Look down through the plastic wrap. The underside of the plastic wrap should be cloudy with moisture. Tap on the plastic wrap. You should see drips of "rain." Remove the ice and plastic wrap, and check the dirt inside the cup. Is it wet? It should be!

HERE'S WHAT'S HAPPENING

You've created a mini-version of Earth's water cycle: The Sun's energy (sunlight or a light bulb) heats liquid water on the Earth's surface (the water in the bowl), causing it to **evaporate** into **water vapor.** The vapor rises into the air until it reaches a cold layer of the **atmosphere** (represented by the ice cube). The cold causes the vapor to **condense** back into liquid and drop back to the Earth's surface (the dirt in the cup) as rain. If not for this water cycle, our planet would become a dry and **barren** place.

FIND OUT MORE

For more information on the science of water, check out these books and Web sites:

BOOKS

Ardley, Neil, and Jack Challoner. *The Science Book of Water.* Steck-Vaughn, 2000.

Challoner, Jack. *Floating and Sinking.* Raintree Steck-Vaughn, 1997.

Ditchfield, Christin; Jan Jenner; and Nanci R. Vargus. *Water.* Scholastic, 2001.

Gardner, Robert. *Experimenting with Water.* Dover, 2004.

Gibbons, Gail, and Dave Gibbons. *Caves and Caverns.* Harcourt, 1996.

Kerley, Barbara. *A Cool Drink of Water.* National Geographic Society, 2002.

Rodgers, Alan, and Angela Streluk. *Precipitation.* Heinemann, 2002.

Zoehfeld, Kathleen Weidner, and Paul Meisel. *What Is The World Made Of?: All about Solids, Liquids, and Gases.* Turtleback Books, 1998.

WEB SITES

American Cave Museum & Hidden River Cave
www.cavern.org/hrc/hrchome.php
A journey through the American Cave Museum is a step into an unknown terrain where nature sculpts enormous subterranean chambers out of limestone. Explore this fascinating world of caves and groundwater through photographs, informative exhibits, and tour videos.

Geography4Kids.com:Hydrosphere
www.geography4kids.com/files/water_
hydrosphere.html
This site from Geography4Kids welcomes you to something called the hydrosphere, and shows you the way water moves through the world. There's water everywhere—in the air, on land, between rocks, and in every living thing.

The Water Cycle (Water Science Basics Web site from USGS)
ga.water.usgs.gov/edu/followdrip.html
Follow a drip of water from ocean to cloud and back to Earth again at this kid-friendly site from the U.S. Geological Survey.

Water Discovery Box
imnh.isu.edu/waterdiscoverybox/
"A world of wondrous water" can be discovered if one looks into the Water Discovery Box created by the Idaho Museum of Natural History.

WonderNet—Solutions
www.chemistry.org/portal/a/c/s/1/wondernetdisplay.
html?DOC=wondernet%5Cactivities%5C
solutions%5Csolutions.html
You've probably dissolved some type of solid, such as sugar or salt, in water. Did you know that liquids and gases can also dissolve? Try some activities to learn more about dissolving and why it is important. From the American Chemical Society.

WonderNet—Surface Tension
www.chemistry.org/portal/a/c/s/1/wondernetdisplay.
html?DOC=wondernet%5Cactivities%5Cwater%5C
water.html
This site focuses on water and surface tension. Try out some fun activities to learn about the interesting properties of this vital substance. From the American Chemical Society.

GLOSSARY

A

absorbs soaks up or takes in.

atmosphere the mixture of gases that surrounds a planet.

B

ballast a weight that helps control the position of a ship or diver.

barren producing little or no vegetation; farmers cannot grow crops on land that is barren.

buoyancy an object's ability to keep afloat.

C

compensators things that provide a balancing effect.

condense to change from a gas into a liquid.

crystals bodies that form a pattern of many flat surfaces when they become a solid. Salt and snowflakes are examples of crystals.

D

dense, density how heavy or light an object is for its size.

displaces takes the place of something or somebody else.

distilled water

distilled water water that's been purified by heating until it turns into a gas and is then cooled to form a liquid again. In this process, all minerals are removed.

E

energy power, or the ability to make something change or move. Forms of energy include light, heat, and electricity.

Epsom salts a mixture of magnesium, sulfur, and oxygen; a mineral sold in drugstores.

evaporate to transform a liquid into a gas.

F

freezing point the temperature at which a liquid freezes. Water freezes at 32° F (0° C). Melting point is the temperature at which ice becomes a liquid. Water melts when the temperature is above 32° F (0° C).

G

gases substances, such as air, that will spread to fill any space that contains them.

H

hard water water hardness relates to the amount of minerals dissolved in water. Soft water has fewer minerals, whereas hard water has more minerals.

humidity moisture in the air.

hygrometer a device to measure humidity.

L

limestone a hard rock formed from the remains of shells or coral.

liquid one of three states of matter; liquids flow and take the shape of their containers.

M

matter anything that has weight and takes up space, such as a solid, a liquid, or a gas.

minerals substances found in nature that are not animals or plants. Gold, salt, and copper are all examples of minerals.

molecules the smallest possible particles of a substance that display all the chemical properties of that substance.

S

soft water water hardness relates to the amount of minerals dissolved in water. Soft water has fewer minerals, whereas hard water has more minerals.

stalactite and stalagmite deposits that resemble icicles, cylinders, or cones and are formed by dripping mineral water (containing mostly calcium carbonate); stalactites project down from the roof of a cave, whereas stalagmites project up from the cave's floor.

T

traction the friction or gripping power that keeps a moving body from slipping on a surface.

V

volume the amount of space occupied by an object.

W

water vapor the gas produced when water evaporates.

iNDEX

Pictures are shown in **bold**.

Photographs © 2008: Getty Images: 26, 20 (Altrendo Travel), 3 middle right, 5 center, 21 (Tom Bean), 29 (Tony Generico), 12 (Jason Hawkes), 5 right center, 16 bottom (Jeff Hunter), cover inner image (Ryan McVay), 5 far left (Philippe Poulet/Mission), 15 (Philippe Poulet/Mission), cover outer image, 1 top (Rubberball Productions), 3 bottom left, 16 top left (Leigh Schindler); Paul Beesley/Shiphotos: 14 top; Photo Researchers, NY: 6 (Martyn F. Chillmaid/Science Photo Library), 1 bottom (Tony McConnell/Science Photo Library), 18 (Science Source), 10 (Charles D. Winter/Science Photo Library); PhotoEdit/David Young-Wolff: 23; Richard Hutchings Photography: back cover, 3 bottom right, 3 middle left, 3 top left, 3 top right, 4 far left, 4 far right, 4 center, 4 left center, 5 left center, 5 far right, 7 top right, 7 top left, 7 bottom, 9, 11, 13 top, 14 bottom, 16 top right, 17, 19, 22, 24, 25, 27, 28, 31 center, 31 left, 31 right; The Image Works: 13 bottom (Roger-Viollet), 8 top (Mitch Wojnarowicz/Amsterdam Recorder).